Wildflower Fantasies

Hannah Dudleson

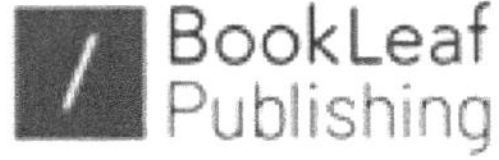

Presentation by *BookLeaf Publishing*

Web: www.bookleafpub.com

E-mail: info@bookleafpub.com

ISBN : 9789357211086

First edition 2022

DEDICATION

To Dad, the reason I picked up a pen all those years ago.

Your Wings Fall Off

Your wings fall off.
The fires are calling,
Heaven's angels scoff.
Your wings fall off.
Feathers no longer soft,
Bare bone appalling,
Your wings fall off.
The fires are calling.

The Newborn Tomb

The forest green and flowers soft below,
The wind moves through, its power yet
channeled.
Rain drifts up from the new dewy meadow,
A scene, serene, not to be dismantled.
Flowers dancing softly in the distance,
Petals a canopy of youth and love,
Blue flowers gladly guiding existence,
Their scent showering down from up above.
The funeral dirge does not distract the dance,
Nor do the tears that from the mourner's flow,
The forest does not even spare a glance
For the body being buried below.
The dancing continues, the flowers bloom,
The rain drifting up from the newborn tomb.

Holiday Drinks

3

Sparkling cider can make you tipsy.
If combined with hallmark
And mismatched socks.
I had a hot latte then,
With cinnamon and hope.
The ball dropped
And I was wearing short sleeves.
What a perfect beginning.
Too bad country fried chicken
And lofts painted white
Aren't the fabric
Holding our lives together.

12:42 a.m.

12:42 a.m. is my favorite time of the day.
You can find me sitting in bed,
The blinds on my windows are usually up.
I like to see the sky, you see.
The moon, especially.
How it bleeds silver, trickling down through
The scarred stars in the sky.
It's familiar. Comforting.
My family's asleep. I'm the only night owl.
I wonder what would happen if all the
Silver trickled out of the moon?
But it never does.
During the day, the moon sneaks out
To replenish itself.
It'll come back though, at night.
Just like me.
12:42 a.m. is quiet and I'm okay with that.
The silver is really pretty.
One of my favorite colors, I think.
It's the same color as the moon.
Looks like stars, with their little indents
And patterns in the sky.
12:42 a.m. is my favorite time of the night.

Workshop

5

The music softly drips through the room
Highlighted by the scratching pens.
Sunlight casting a soft spell
As it plays with the steam
Rising from hot tea.
The wood desk creaks
From the weight
Of thoughts
Held.

What if He Won't Take It?

Now I lay me down to sleep,
I pray the Lord my soul to keep,
But what if he doesn't want it?

I've sinned a lot inside by head
With friends, myself, and in my bed,
So what if he won't take it?

"Jesus Saves," my pastor calls,
His voice echoing through the church halls,
The people around me shower hearty applause,
But I can hardly believe it.

"No height, no depth, no scheme of man
Can ever pluck me from his hand."
I am clay in the potters hand,
A product of his master plan,
But I just wish I could feel it.

I have to believe nothing I can do
No sin, no act, no harm I'll do
Can ever take me away from you,
No, never take me away from you,
Jesus, help me believe this.

Your consuming, flaming, perfect love

Poured out on me from heaven above
Will take away my scarlet sins
And give me a new heart where your spirit lives.

But God, how could you ever want me?
With my flaws and scars, will you ever choose
me?
Please take my heart and create within me
A new heart where your spirit lives,
I want a heart where your spirit lives.
Jesus, help me receive it.

A Trilogy of Twisted Nursery Rhymes

Hickory Dickory Dock,
Keep your eyes fixed on the clock,
If the hand gets to one
The world will be done
And eternally frozen in shock.

Twinkle twinkle little star,
Torches on the lake afar.
FIre demons burning bright,
Hands are all pinned down in fright.
Sudden darkness rolling in,
Tripping over my dead friend.

Here is the church
Blood on the steeple
Bang on the doors
Crushed by the people.

Goodness

I feel lost in the moment
And not in a good way,
Then I see your face
And you tell me to stay.
"I love you," I think to myself,
But only for today.
Because when the morning comes
Your goodness fades away.

Bravery, Courage, Honor

The world tells you to drown everyone out,
Says they'll applaud anyone who stands
Against the mainstream,
Holds outcasts and rebels on a golden
Pedestal.
Then it'll tear you down for
believing in your own ideals.

Bravery isn't doing what everyone
tells you to,
Courage isn't going with the crowd,
Honor should not be destruction,
So use your voices, raise them loud.

A Modern-Day Fairytale

Once upon a time
The princess was kidnapped
By an evil wizard.
He chained her in his castle.

The princess was kidnapped
But no one else could tell.
He chained her in his castle,
She seemed just fine.

No one could tell,
She was the same girl,
She seemed just fine.
The wizard watched her every move.

She was the same girl,
But her eyes were a thunderstorm.
The wizard watched her every move,
And she had no escape.

Her eyes were a thunderstorm,
Her hands were bound in his dungeon
She could find no escape,
He laughed through it all.

Her hands were bound in his dungeon,

The ticking clocks echoed the years.
The years of him laughing through it all,
It happened once upon a time.

Void

I call out into the void
But this time it answers back.
And I should be surprised, but I'm not
Because there should be a new law
Of nature
That says the more you cry
The better your chances of being heard are.
So it answers me,
Not audibly, but I can feel it.
Paralyzing and hypnotizing.
Reshaping my mind like
Its own personal Frankenstein.
Reaching into my brain
And pulling it inside out.
Beginning a redemption arc
That stretches across my entire brain;
Conscious and subconscious.
It's intrusive but comforting.
Foreign, yet welcome,
And my hands feel like they can shoot
White healing fire.
And then I am jolted awake.
Disoriented and lost,
Confused and alone,
My comfort gone,
My mind at home.

Stupid Little Name

I have a little red book
With a little list of names,
And yours is circled once
Then time and time again.

One little circle
For every tear I've shed,
And a couple more
For those sleepless nights in bed.

The inks a little smudged
Where I poured out my anger,
A few little places where
I ripped it with my finger.

And fumed at your name
Wished I could cut my eyes out.
Delete every memory
And replace them with a shout.

Now this story's over,
It wasn't very long.
Because I don't care enough about you
For a single heartbreak song.

Wildflower

One day, I tried to write a poem about a girl.
A girl with an amber wildfire in her eyes,
Flames licking up-and-down,
Cracking and popping with every motion of
Her fluid body.
One day, I tried to write a poem about a girl
Who wore a dress made of wildflowers,
Wildflowers that ruffled back-and-forth
With every breeze,
Wildflowers that hugged her body like a
Mother hugs her newborn baby.
One day, I tried to write a poem about a girl
Whose voice sounded like a running brook,
A brook that babbled so smoothly and
Beautifully,
Carrying her along with it,
Filtering out all the sharp sticks and rocks,
And leaving the beautiful water in its wake.
But the thing about wildfires is that they
Can be put out with one gush of water,
One unkind bucket full of dirty liquid,
Not the water that came from her mouth
So beautifully,
But the water that's green and murky and
Full of the unknown,
The water that can wash away all the good

And the beautiful and leave the sludge and
Mud in its place.
The problem with wildflowers is that it
Takes one swift cut to get rid of them all,
One little nip and they're gone forever,
Never to grow back.
The thing about water is that it's so easily
Diverted,
With just a dam, a few sticks pasted
Together with that ugly mud that hurts so
Much.
So the poem didn't turn out very well
Because everything that was good and
Beautiful was torn down in a matter of
Seconds,
With one unkind and unthought out
Sentence, the whole poem crumbled,
And with it the girl with the amber wildfire
Eyes,
Wildfire dress,
And beautiful babbling words.

Fire

I am a masterpiece.
A product of design,
Crafted, Creative, Fire.

Passionately made to shout.
Shout glory, shout praise.
A designed and perfect person.

A firebomb that can destroy,
A firework that can shower love,
A haunted creation of glory.

We are all fire.
Choose your flame wisely
And you will never burn out.

God's Plan

18

Truly Redeemed
Unendingly Perfected
Loved Forever
Incomparably Created
Perfectly Planned

Fight and Flight

19

Fight or flight,
All I can think of are small-town dreams.
Noose on neck, knife in hands
When you're here, they'll never take me.
Kiss me through the fire,
You'll never be a liar,
Hanging out a window but
Your reflection's looking back at me.

8 Words

The brain is a muddled pool of thoughts.
Colorful threads of thought run in all directions.
Red anger, spilling and knotted together with blue.
Blue, the beautiful serenity of accepting the unacceptable.
A yellow thread flies overhead-whispy and carefree.
Blue and green-acceptance and logic-tangling irrevocably.
Purple in the corner-happiness finally resolving itself.
The threads run together in the middle and stop.
God calmly smoothing and untangling every single one.

Group Therapy

One says spiders,
Another says snakes.
Someone's voice trembles,
Her shoulders shake.

"Loss," says another,
"Me too!" someone cries.
Death or the void,
Having no place to hide.

Tight spaces too,
And towering heights.
The dark underwater,
Airplane flights.

Then you speak
You say you're hard to grasp.
You want to wait,
Just go last.

Your one greatest fear
Isn't one you can see.
It's deep on the inside
And you've only shared it with me.

A Very Bad Love Song

Coffee shop haze,
Roasted beans and whipped cream.
The wilted flowers on my table
Forming an umbrella over my page,
The scent masking the smell
Of burnt toast.

Math homework is piling up,
But I'd rather sip my coffee
And write about you.
Just for once
Spread positivity,
Not bad dreams.

I'm not good at writing affection,
So I'll just sip my coffee
Watch the clock tick
And wish you sweet dreams.

Your Bad Side

I want to make you happy
But I have to save some time for me.
Going out of my way to check on you,
Just ignore me again
Like you always do.
You seem full of sweetness and goodness,
So I'll trust you this once
To see what will happen
And if you'll hurt me.
I don't mind being left out
If you'll be up front in the spotlight.
Don't force me to be on the hunt
For clues that you're upset.
I'm so sick of unexplained endings,
Abrupt goodbyes, and messages not sending.

www.ingramcontent.com/pod-product-compliance
Lightning Source LLC
Chambersburg PA
CBHW070732160726
48003CB00006BA/2457